Contents

Any words appearing in bold, **like this**, are explained in the Glossary

Introduction

Stringed instruments have a very long history in most cultures throughout the world. One instrument, a **bow** with a **resonator** attached, which originated in Africa, is probably one of the very oldest musical instruments of all.

The symphony orchestra is split into sections. This is the violin section of the strings.

Bowed strings...

Today, there are an enormous number of different stringed instruments in use in all kinds of music throughout the world. In European and American classical music, the violin, viola, cello and double **bass** make up the string section of the **symphony orchestra**. They are also played in other, smaller classical music groups. The violin is also used extensively in various folk musics, as well as having been adopted into Indian classical music (where it is sometimes played upright on the player's lap), and both the violin and the double bass are used in jazz. A string section is also a popular choice as backing for some rock and pop music.

...plucked and stopped strings...

The guitar is possibly the most widely-recognized musical instrument in the world today. The classical guitar, which originally had strings made from animal gut but now usually has nylon strings, is an important instrument in its family. Some steel-strung guitars were developed from the classical guitar, including the various types of **acoustic** guitar used in folk, jazz and acoustic rock music. When the steel-strung guitar was

SOUNDBITES

Strings

Roger Thomas

www.heinemann.co.uk/library
Visit our website to find out more information about Heinemann Library books.

To order:
☎ Phone 44 (0) 1865 888066
🖹 Send a fax to 44 (0) 1865 314091
💻 Visit the Heinemann Bookshop at www.heinemann.co.uk/library to browse our catalogue and order online.

First published in Great Britain by Heinemann Library, Halley Court, Jordan Hill, Oxford, OX2 8EJ, a division of Reed Educational and Professional Publishing Ltd.
Heinemann is a registered trademark of Reed Educational and Professional Publishing Ltd.

OXFORD MELBOURNE AUCKLAND
JOHANNESBURG BLANTYRE GABORONE
IBADAN PORTSMOUTH NH (USA) CHICAGO

Designed by Paul Davies and Associates
Originated by Ambassador Litho Ltd.
Printed at Wing King Tong in Hong Kong

ISBN 0 431 13072 8 (hardback)   ISBN 0 431 13079 5 (paperback)
06 05 04 03 02   06 05 04 03 02
10 9 8 7 6 5 4 3 2   10 9 8 7 6 5 4 3 2 1

British Library Cataloguing in Publication Data

Thomas, Roger, 1956-
    Strings. - (Soundbites)
    1.Stringed instruments - Juvenile literature 2.Stringed
    instrument music - Juvenile literature
    I.Title
    787

Acknowledgements

The Publishers would like to thank the following for permission to reproduce photographs: Corbis: Pg.15, Pg.16; Lebrecht Picture Library: Pg.6, Pg.9, Pg.18, Pg.21, Pg.26; Musicmaker's Kits Inc.: Pg.20; Outline Press: Pg.28; Photodisc: Pg.5, Pg.7, Pg.12, Pg.14; Redferns: Pg.4, Pg.8, Pg.11, Pg.13, Pg.17, Pg.22, Pg.24, Pg.25, Pg.27; Robert Harding Picture Library: Pg.19; South American Pictures: Pg.23; The New Violin Family Assoc. Inc.: Pg.29; Trevor Clifford: Pg.10.

Cover photograph reproduced with permission of Redferns/Outline.

Our thanks to Jennifer Baker for her comments in the preparation of this book.

Every effort has been made to contact copyright holders of any material reproduced in this book. Any omissions will be rectified in subsequent printings if notice is given to the publishers.

modified with **electromagnetic pickups**, the result was the electric guitar, the most important instrument in rock and pop music, and perhaps the most important musical instrument of the 20th century.

The guitar is related to an earlier instrument called the **lute**, which in turn was developed from an Arabic instrument, the oud. The lute is also related to various other European and Middle Eastern instruments, such as the Greek **bouzouki**. The banjo, the ukelele and the mandolin are all very different instruments which originated in completely different parts of the world, yet they all work on the same basic principle as the lute and guitar. The notes made by these instruments are changed by '**stopping**' – a string being held down onto the **neck** with one hand, while the other hand plucks the string to sound the notes. Each of these instruments is used in music of its own particular culture, but they can also be used in lots of other different kinds of music. For example, the bouzouki is now popular in English folk music.

Harps and lyres are also played by plucking. Their strings are not stopped by the player's fingers but are allowed to vibrate along their full length.

...hammered strings and blown strings

These methods are also used for playing stringed instruments – but you'll have to wait until later in the book to find out more!

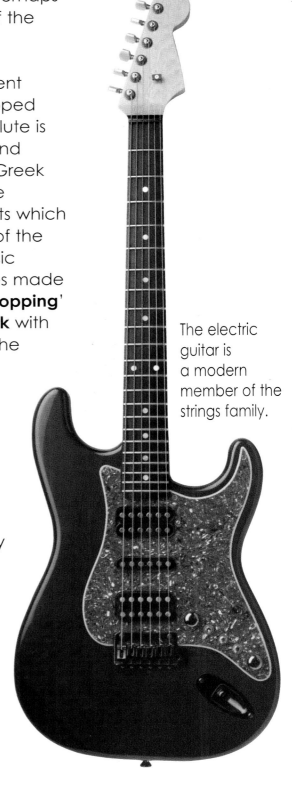

The electric guitar is a modern member of the strings family.

How stringed instruments work

All stringed instruments, throughout history and throughout the world, work in the same way. One or more strings is stretched between two firm anchor points on the instrument, then tightened so that, when plucked, rubbed or struck, the string vibrates. We hear this vibration as sound.

Strings and soundboxes

Most strings are not loud enough to be heard clearly on their own. For this reason, most stringed instruments also include some form of **resonator**, or **soundbox**, which is usually some sort of empty box attached to the instrument – it is not really empty, it is full of air. While the string does not vibrate powerfully enough for us to hear it very loudly by itself, it is powerful enough to vibrate the air in the soundbox. The sound that we hear is the sound of the vibrating air added to the sound of the string.

There are some exceptions to this. The simplest form of musical **bow** does not have a resonator attached, but the player provides one by placing one end of the bow in his or her mouth. Some zithers (see pages 18–19) have detachable soundboxes. Electric guitars, electric **bass** guitars and other electrically **amplified** string instruments often have solid bodies instead of soundboxes. These do resonate to a certain extent, but the sound is then amplified electronically so that it is loud enough for musical performance.

The viol can be traced back to the beginning of the 15th century. It is played with a bow but, unlike the violin family, has **frets** to help in producing accurate notes.

Tuning and melody

Stringed instruments usually have some sort of mechanism built into them for tightening their strings. One of the simplest methods is to simply pull the string as tight as possible, then to slide one or more objects under the string which will lift it away from the instrument and pull it even tighter at the same time. This method is used on an instrument found in Africa and South-East Asia called a ground zither, which is a string stretched across a bark-covered pit dug into the ground. Most other instruments have rotating pegs at one end of each string. Some, like the violin and many folk harps, have wooden pegs which are fitted tightly into holes. Others, such as the guitar and double bass, have a system of metal **gears** to tighten the string smoothly. Some others, such as the **psaltery**, have a spanner-like key to tighten the strings.

There are several different ways of reaching a range of notes on a stringed instrument. There can be a string for each note, as with the Arab **qanun**; the strings may be stretched while playing, as with the concert harp and some types of electric guitar; the strings can be 'shortened' by **stopping**, as with most guitars, or by pressing an object against them, as with the steel or Hawaiian guitar; or **harmonics** can be used, as with the Egyptian folk harp.

The violin (shown here) and viola are very similar. Neither have frets, but the viola is slightly larger and **pitched** lower.

The parts of a stringed instrument

Neck or no neck?

Instruments without **necks**, such as the harp and dulcimer, consist of strings stretched across a frame or box. Instruments with necks include the guitar, the **bass** guitar, the banjo, the violin, the viola, the cello, the double bass and many others. Each has a similar set of parts which have the same function, although they may be used for very different kinds of music. The easiest way to identify the parts is to follow the strings from one end of the instrument to the other.

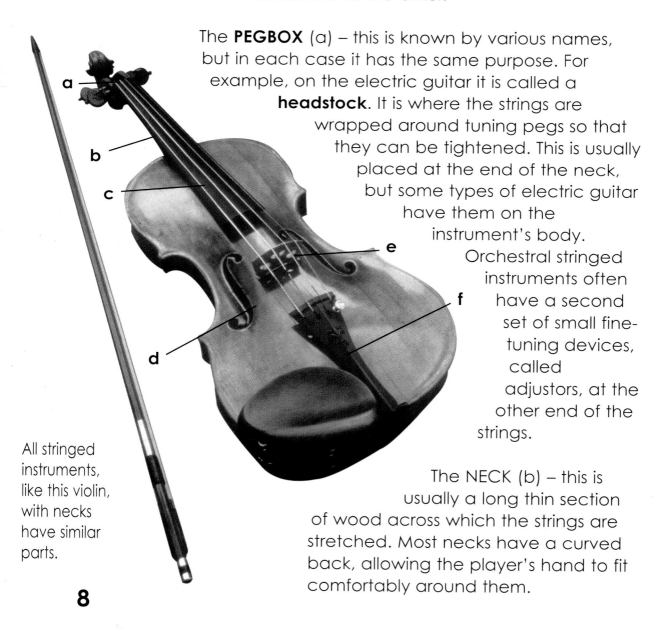

The **PEGBOX** (a) – this is known by various names, but in each case it has the same purpose. For example, on the electric guitar it is called a **headstock**. It is where the strings are wrapped around tuning pegs so that they can be tightened. This is usually placed at the end of the neck, but some types of electric guitar have them on the instrument's body. Orchestral stringed instruments often have a second set of small fine-tuning devices, called adjustors, at the other end of the strings.

The NECK (b) – this is usually a long thin section of wood across which the strings are stretched. Most necks have a curved back, allowing the player's hand to fit comfortably around them.

All stringed instruments, like this violin, with necks have similar parts.

The **FINGERBOARD** (c) – this is a smooth piece of wood, usually on the front of the neck. The player presses the strings down onto this to change the notes. The fingerboard on this type of stringed instrument may or may not have **frets**. On the guitar family, they are small strips of wire attached to the fingerboard. Other instruments, such as the violin family, have no frets. The related viol family, however, does have frets. Frets have two effects on the instrument. Firstly, they make the notes very accurate, as the string is always pulled onto the fret in the same position. Secondly, they prevent the player's fingertips from muffling the sound of the string, which can make the **tone** of the instrument clearer and brighter.

Stringed instruments with and without necks may be used for very different kinds of music, but both have similar parts which have the same function.

The **SOUNDBOX** (d) – this hollow box which **amplifies** the sound is present on most non-electric stringed instruments.

The **BRIDGE** (e) and **TAILPIECE** (f) – the bridge is the point at which the strings are pulled over a hard edge to give a precise point beyond which they cannot vibrate. The strings may then be attached to a tailpiece on the end of the instrument, or anchored behind the bridge.

The violin and the viola

The violin and the viola are the highest and second-highest **pitched** stringed instruments in the classical orchestra. The violin is used in many other forms of music, including jazz and folk music, and there are many instruments similar to the violin in use in different musical cultures across the world. They are played with a **bow** which has a length of horsehair (or a man-made substitute) attached along its length. A sticky substance called **rosin** is rubbed onto the horsehair, which then causes the strings to vibrate when the bow is drawn across them. The instruments are held under the player's chin.

The violin and viola in classical music

These two instruments are used in several different ways in classical music. Here are some examples:

- The ORCHESTRA – there are two sections of violins in the **symphony orchestra**, known as the first and second violins. Each section has a different part to play. There is also a form of music called the **concerto**, in which an instrumental **soloist** is featured with an orchestra. There are many concertos written for the violin and some for the viola, too.

The viola has a lower pitch than the violin, but is played in a similar way.

Yehudi Menuhin, a **virtuoso** violin player.

- The **CHAMBER** GROUP – this is a smaller group of instrumentalists, which may feature one or more violins and/or violas together with other instruments. There are also smaller groups for string players, such as the **string quartet**, which usually includes two violins, one viola and a cello.
- The SONATA – the sonata is a work for a single instrument, generally with piano accompaniment. Many sonatas have been written for the violin, and some for the viola.

Jazz, rock, folk and world music

The violin can also be used in traditional jazz, 'fusion' (a cross between jazz and rock music) and in **avant-garde** jazz. The viola, with its deeper, 'darker' sound, is not popular in these areas of music. However, this quality has meant that some rock bands, such as The Velvet Underground, found the viola to be an interesting addition to their sound. The violin is sometimes used in rock music, either as a solo instrument (mostly in electric 'folk-rock') or as part of a string section backing a rock band, which may also include violas. The violin is also used extensively in 'pure' folk music forms, ranging from **Cajun** to **Gaelic** music. The European violin has also become an important instrument in Indian music.

Electric instruments

The use of the violin in non-classical music has led to the development of electric violins with solid bodies like most electric guitars. One, designed by the Indian violinist L. Shankar, has two **necks** with different tunings.

The cello and the double bass

The cello and the double **bass** play the second-lowest and lowest range of notes in the string section of a **symphony** or **chamber orchestra**. Like the violin and viola (see pages 10–11), they are also used in other forms of classical music, including the **concerto**, the sonata and in chamber **ensembles**.

Unlike the violin and viola, however, these instruments are played vertically. A cellist normally sits on a chair, holding the body of the instrument between his or her knees, with the weight of the instrument resting on a spike. The double bass is a larger instrument, and a classical player will usually sit on a high stool to play it. The body of the double bass rests on the floor on a small support attached to the bottom of the instrument. Occasionally the player may choose to stand while playing the instrument. This playing position is also popular with jazz bassists.

The spike supporting the cello can be adjusted to the height needed by the cellist.

Bowed and plucked

In classical music, both the cello and the double bass are usually played with a **bow**, although occasionally there will be parts of the music where the strings have to be plucked with the fingers. This technique is called **pizzicato**, and is also used by classical violin and viola players. Jazz bassists, on the other hand, are more often required to play their instrument by plucking and slapping the strings than by using a bow. For this reason, many jazz players keep the bow in a holster attached to the instrument.

Variations

The cello has not altered very much since it first began to replace an earlier instrument, the *bass viola de bracchio*, in the early 1600s. However, these early cellos had five strings, whereas the modern cello has four.

The double bass, however, has been experimented with in many different ways. Although the cello and the double bass look similar, the double bass was developed from the viol family rather than the *viola de bracchio*. Many double basses have lower 'shoulders' which are more like the bass viol than the violin family. Some versions of the double bass have five strings, instead of

Double basses are popular with jazz artists.

four. There are also devices which can be attached to the **pegbox** to allow one of the strings to be slightly longer, so that deeper notes can be played.

Electric instruments

Some manufacturers have made electric cellos, including one folding model designed for use at home. However, various types of electric double bass have existed since the 1950s. Some have bodies which are completely or partly hollow, in which case they can look fairly similar to the standard double bass (although they are often finished in very bright colours), whereas solid-bodied instruments can have unusual shapes. These instruments are usually used by jazz and rock musicians, many of whom started out by playing the bass guitar.

Fretted instruments

There is a huge number of **fretted** instruments in use across the world. The guitar is one of the most important, as this instrument alone is made in many designs.

Types of guitar

* The CLASSICAL GUITAR is used to play **solo**, **ensemble** and **concerto** music from the classical **repertoire**. It usually has six nylon strings (some models have more than this) which are plucked with the fingertips and nails. Earlier versions, such as the smaller **Baroque** guitar, are still used for playing period music.

* The FOLK GUITAR is also known simply as the **acoustic** guitar, to distinguish it from the electric guitar. It is similar to the Spanish guitar but is often larger and has steel strings. It is often played with a **plectrum**. Variations include a twelve-string version, a version with a curved, plastic body and a version with a metal plate on the front of the body which gives the instrument a sharp, cutting tone.

* The ARCHTOP or CELLO GUITAR. This type of guitar looks a little like a cello, in that it has a **neck** tilted away from the body and has 'f'shaped sound holes. It was designed to replace the banjo in dance bands, and is popular as a jazz instrument.

- The ELECTRIC GUITAR is used mainly in rock, pop and jazz music, and is one of the most popular guitars in the world. The sound of the strings is transmitted by **electronic pickups** to an **amplifier**. Most have solid bodies, but there are also electric archtop guitars with full-sized or slightly shallower hollow bodies which are most popular as jazz instruments.
- The **BASS** GUITAR plays lower notes than the electric guitar and has thicker, heavier strings. Traditionally the bass guitar has four strings (like the double bass, as it was originally invented as an alternative to that instrument), but there are versions with five, six or even more strings, as well as smaller 'short-scale' designs which some players prefer. There are electric and acoustic types. There are also models with no frets, which have a similar tone to the double bass.

The Chinese mandolin is one among a huge variety of fretted instruments in use across the world.

Other fretted instruments

These include the banjo, which has a drum-like body; the mandolin, which is like a small, steel-strung **lute**; the mandola, which is like a large mandolin; the Indian sitar, which has large, movable frets, and the ukelele, a Hawaiian instrument which looks like a small, four-string Spanish guitar (the name means 'dancing flea'!). There are also combination instruments such as the banjolin and banjolele, which have a banjo-like body, but a neck and strings like the mandolin and the ukelele respectively.

Innovative instruments

New fretted instruments are still being invented. These have included the sitar-guitar, which is a guitar with a sitar-like tone, and the Chapman Stick, an electric instrument which is played by 'hammering' the strings against the frets with the fingers.

15

Harps and lyres

This is a very ancient group of instruments. Pictures of harps and lyres have been found on fragments of pottery dating back to 3300 BCE. There have been many variations and refinements in the design of these instruments over the centuries, but their working principles remain the same.

Harp or lyre?

The main difference between a harp and a lyre is in the way each is made. A harp is basically triangular in shape, whereas a lyre is a rectangle. On a harp, the strings run from one side of the triangle to another. On a lyre, the strings run from one of the rectangle to the opposite end. On both harps and lyres, one end of the strings is usually attached to a **soundbox** which forms a part of the instrument.

Lyres

Various forms of lyre were played in Europe during the Middle Ages, often as an accompaniment to singing. Most were plucked, but a few, like the Welsh crwth, were played with a **bow**. However, the lyre has survived in only a few cultures, such as in Africa, where many different designs are played in Egypt, the Sudan, Kenya, Uganda and elsewhere.

A lyre is an ancient instrument, with strings that run from one end of its rectangular shape to the other.

Types of harp

- The CONCERT or PEDAL HARP. This is the type of harp usually used for performances of classical music. It is used in symphony orchestras, in some **chamber ensembles**, as a **solo** instrument (including concertos) and as an accompanying instrument. The strings, which the player plucks with his or her fingers, are tuned at the top of the instrument. The soundbox is at the bottom of the instrument. There is a set of pedals at the base of the instrument which can change the **tension** of the strings, which makes a wider range of notes available.

- The CLARSACH. This is a traditional Celtic harp which originated in Ireland. It has a similar shape to the concert harp, but is smaller, has fewer strings and no pedals. It is sometimes used as an instrument for people who want to learn how to play the concert harp. Its name means 'little flat thing', despite the fact that it is vertical and quite large!

- DOUBLE and TRIPLE HARPS. These were early attempts to allow the harp to play more notes, before the invention of the pedal harp. They were developed during the 16th and 17th centuries. The double harp had two rows of strings, each with a different tuning. The triple harp had two outer sets of strings with the same tuning, with a middle set of strings tuned to the 'missing' notes. This made it easier to reach all the correct notes with either hand.

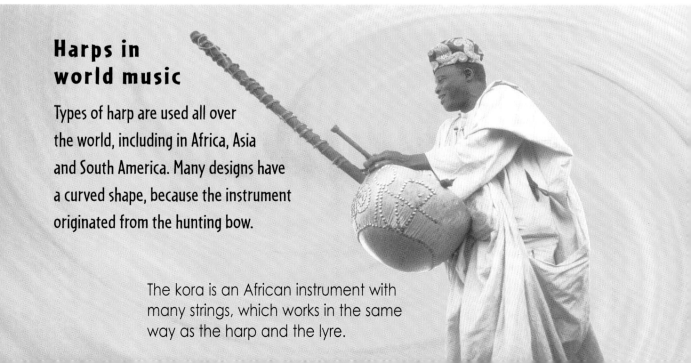

Harps in world music

Types of harp are used all over the world, including in Africa, Asia and South America. Many designs have a curved shape, because the instrument originated from the hunting bow.

The kora is an African instrument with many strings, which works in the same way as the harp and the lyre.

Zithers

Zithers are types of stringed instruments on which the strings run from one end to the other, often (but not always) with no **frets** or other means of changing the note of a single string. These instruments are played by plucking. They are similar to dulcimers (see pages 20–21), except that dulcimers are usually played with hammers.

Simple zithers

The most simple zithers illustrate the most important principles of stringed instruments very well. In Africa, there are trough zithers, which are made of a hollowed-out piece of wood with strings stretched across the hollow area. The result looks like an animal feeding trough, hence the name. Sometimes one long continuous string is used, stretched backwards and forwards across the trough. Tube zithers are traditional in some parts of Africa and Eastern Europe. They can be made of wood or cane and usually consist of a single hollow cylinder with a slot cut in it to let the sound out.

Some zithers are very sophisticated. The vina, an Indian instrument, comes in several different designs. The most basic consists of a hollow tube with strings stretched along it and a **gourd soundbox** at one end. There are other types which have many strings and frets.

The Japanese koto is another type of zither with a very distinctive sound.

One or two strings are then tied to the ends of the instrument, with a small **bridge** placed under each end of the string to give a clear sound (see pages 8–9). On some tube zithers, the 'string' is formed from the material which has been cut for the slot. It is left attached at each end of the slot, and small bridges are forced underneath it to raise and tighten the 'string'.

Not-so-simple zithers

The Japanese **koto** has movable bridges which can be slid up and down the instrument to change the notes. By pressing a string down on one side of the bridge while plucking it on the other side, the player can raise the pitch of the note slightly. This gives a 'bending' effect similar to that which can be produced on an electric guitar. There are similar instruments to the koto in Korea, such as the kayakeum, and in China, such as the ch'in.

Piggy zithers!

The European zither is usually box shaped and has a set of tuning pegs at one end. It is a popular folk instrument in many countries, especially in Eastern Europe, and has a long history. One very early example is the **psaltery**, which was developed from an Arab zither which was first brought to Europe in the 11th century. One European zither played in the 14th and 15th centuries had a triangular shape with sound holes in each corner. It was said to remind people of a pig's head, and was known as '*strumento di porco*', meaning 'pig instrument'.

Dulcimers

Dulcimers are similar to zithers (see pages 18–19), except that instead of being plucked, the strings are struck with hammers or beaters. This means that the dulcimer is also really a percussion instrument. It also has similarities to two keyboard instruments which work by having strings struck with hammers – the piano and the **clavichord**.

Another Middle-Eastern import

Like the zither, the dulcimer came to Europe from the Middle East in the 11th century. From the 17th to the 19th centuries it was very popular, but it is now mostly used for playing traditional music. Different kinds of dulcimer are found in the musical traditions of many countries, including the Iraqi santir, Russian chang, Indian santoor and the Korean yangum.

A Far-Eastern export

The Chinese yang chin is rather more unusual. Just as the European violin was adopted by Indian musicians, the zither was introduced into China from the West as recently as 1800, where it became absorbed into the Chinese musical tradition. The Chinese name for this instrument actually means 'foreign'.

Not a dulcimer...

The most widely-heard instrument known as a dulcimer today is not really a dulcimer at all, but a type of **fretted** zither. The Appalachian dulcimer is an elegant instrument with a narrow **fretboard**, and the strings are plucked rather than struck. It is used in many several forms of folk music, particularly in America.

The Appalachian dulcimer is a beautiful instrument, which is really a zither.

A classical dulcimer

The cimbalom is a fairly large dulcimer from Hungary. The design of the cimbalom was improved in the 1860s so that it had a wider range of notes. **Dampers** were also added to allow the player to change the **tone** of the instrument. This meant it could be used in classical music, and the composer Kodaly used it in his well-known suite 'Hary Janos' in 1927. In classical music, the job of playing the cimbalom is usually given to a percussionist, as the use of hammers and beaters is a percussion technique.

The cimbalom was originally a Hungarian gypsy folk instrument.

Dulcimer beater

Various different kinds of beaters are used for playing instruments from the dulcimer family, depending on the traditions of the music in which the instrument is going to be used. The three main styles are straight sticks, sticks with curved ends, or sticks with padded ends which give a softer sound. Because the strings give the instrument a very 'bouncy' response, a skilled player can produce very fast and complicated tunes on the instrument.

Does size matter?

At the end of the 17th century, a German musician named Pantaleon Hebenstreit built a very large dulcimer, which became known as the pantaleon. The instrument was eleven feet long, had two soundboards and quadruple sets of strings. He composed several successful works for the instrument.

Other kinds of string instruments

Many of the stringed instruments used in the **West** are based on instruments from other parts of the world, such as the guitar and the **lute**. However, there are many other non-Western stringed instruments which remain unique to the musical cultures in which they originated. Here are a few examples:

- The SITAR and SARANGHI. These two Indian instruments could not be more different. The sitar is the best-known instrument from India. It is a large, lute-like instrument with a bowl-shaped wooden **soundbox** at the bottom and usually another, made from a dried **gourd**, at the top. The sitar has two sets of strings. One set consists of seven strings which the player plucks with a **plectrum**. The notes on five of these strings can be changed by pressing them against movable metal **frets** on the instrument's large **neck**. As with the koto (see page 19), the player can add a 'bending' sound to the notes. The other two strings are '**drone strings**', which means that they are not **stopped** on the frets and will always give the same notes. Beneath these seven strings are twelve or more '**sympathetic strings**', which are not touched by the player but are made to vibrate by the sound of the top set of strings. This gives the instrument its unique sound.

The Indian sitar has a unique sound. This is Ravi Shankar, the famous Indian sitarist.

The charango

When Spanish travellers first reached South America, they brought with them examples of a guitar-like instrument called the vihuela. The native inhabitants copied the idea, but instead of using wood to make the soundbox, they used the shell of a small animal called an armadillo. This version of the instrument, which is still used today by South American folk groups, became known as the charango. Some other types have a more conventional wooden soundbox.

An unlucky armadillo might have been used to make this charango!

The saranghi is a small bowed instrument which is held in front of the player. It also has a set of sympathetic strings. Unusually, the strings are stopped using the cuticles of the player's fingernails.

- The BALALAIKA. Long thought of as the national instrument of Russia, the balalaika was first known in Europe in the 17th century. It is a type of lute, with three strings and an unusual triangular **soundbox**. There are six different sizes, all of which are used in large balalaika bands.

- The PI-PA. One of many Chinese plucked instruments, the pi-pa is a type of lute with a short neck and a distinctive 'teardrop' shape. It has been known in China for about 2000 years. It has four silk strings which produce a warm and clear **tone**.

- The RAMKIE. An interesting example of how modern technology can be adapted to folk instruments, the ramkie is a type of simple, home-made folk guitar played in Southern Africa. Originally, they had soundboxes made from gourds or dried skin, but now tin cans are often used instead.

23

Strings in jazz, rock and pop

The guitar and bass guitar are the most widely used stringed instruments in rock and pop. In jazz, the double **bass** is also widely used. However, there are many other examples of string instruments being used in these forms of music. Here are just a few examples:

- The VIOLIN, VIOLA and CELLO. Together with the double bass, these are sometimes used to put together a complete orchestral string section to provide backing for rock and pop tunes. Sometimes just a **string quartet** (see page 11) will be used. This is an idea which goes in and out of fashion. It was popular during the 1950s and again during the 1990s. The violin, usually **amplified** or in the form of an electric instrument, is popular in electric 'folk-rock' and is also used in jazz. The double bass is sometimes used in rock music in a deliberate 'retro' style, and some rock bassists use a solid-bodied, electric double bass. The whole range of orchestral string instruments can be used in **avant-garde** jazz.
- The SITAR and sitar-like instruments. In the 1960s and 1970s, several rock bands, including the Beatles and

The rock band Nirvana used a string section in some of their performances.

Banjo music

The banjo, which is a bit like a guitar, except that its **soundbox** has a front made of stretched **vellum** or plastic (like a drum), is an instrument which probably evolved from African lyres (see pages 16-17) which worked in a similar way. It has a very bright, loud sound and was used in early dance and jazz bands. Today, the banjo is widely used in folk music in America and elsewhere, and in traditional jazz bands which aim to recreate the sound of early jazz.

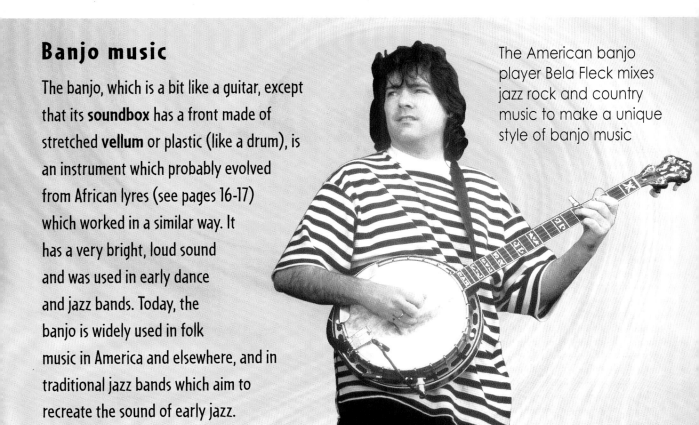

The American banjo player Bela Fleck mixes jazz rock and country music to make a unique style of banjo music

The Rolling Stones, were influenced by Indian music and used a sitar on some of their recordings. One guitar manufacturer made several models of sitar-guitar. These were electric guitars which had **sympathetic strings** (see page 22) and a special **bridge**, enabling them to make a sitar-like sound. These instruments were easier for rock guitarists to play than the sitar.

- The AUTOHARP. This is a type of zither which has sets of **dampers** operated by buttons which **mute** certain strings. By removing notes from the instrument's sound in this way, the player has a set of 'ready-made' chords which can be strummed or plucked. The instrument was often used by folk-rock musicians. More recently, the musician Daniel Lanois has used a form of 'hi-tech' autoharp, which has electronic sensors instead of strings.

- The MANDOLIN. Normally associated with classical and folk music, the mandolin is occasionally used in rock and jazz, and electric mandolins have been developed which work in the same way as the electric guitar.

Strings and recording/performance technology

Although the electric guitar and **bass** are very important in today's music, all stringed instruments began their history as **acoustic** instruments. There are very few exceptions to this rule – the Chapman Stick is one (see page 15). However, the need to project the sound of the instruments to large audiences, together with the invention of sound recording, meant that electronic technology has had an important place in the history of this family of instruments.

An early solution

Before the invention of electronic recording, music was recorded by placing a very large funnel-like horn in front of the musicians. The horn tapered down to a point which had a sharp needle on it. The needle vibrated when music was played into the horn, cutting a groove into a 'master' disc (a wax cylinder was used for the earliest recordings). However, the delicate sound of stringed instruments did not record well in this way. So in 1904, German inventor Augustus Stroh

Using microphones means that it is now possible to record the sound of string instruments much more clearly.

created a violin with a metal trumpet-like horn instead of a **soundbox**, which could project the sound straight into the recording horn. However, the **tone** of the instrument was not very good.

Strings and microphones

The microphone and electronic recording made it possible to record stringed instruments much more accurately. Various techniques have been used for recording orchestral string sections, ranging from placing a microphone above each instrument to simply placing one or two microphones in front of all the performers. Acoustic guitars and other **solo** string instruments are usually recorded with one or two microphones placed near the instrument, but for live performance, a type of microphone which is attached directly to the instrument is often used. This is called a transducer, and is much less likely to pick up sound from outside the instrument. Some musicians use both techniques at once and mix the results, which gives a pleasing sound.

The electric guitar

The electric guitar relies on **amplification** in performance. However, in the early days of the instrument, the amplifiers available would often produce feedback (where the sound from the amplifier is picked up by the guitar, producing a howling noise) and a distorted sound. Guitarists began to make use of these 'faults' as an interesting aspect of their instrument's sound. Many modern amplifiers do not produce feedback, but there are electronic devices, often built into boxes with footswitches, which will produce this and many other changes to the guitar's sound electronically.

Electronic technology can be as important to the electric guitarist as the instrument itself.

Innovative strings

Stringed instruments are quite simply constructed in comparison with, for example, the mechanism of the piano or the valve system of a brass instrument. This makes them easy to modify, and may be one reason why there have been so many different ideas for creating more ways for stringed instruments to make sounds. A few of these ideas are described below.

More necks, more strings

Some early **fretted** instruments, such as the theorbo (a form of **bass lute**) had extra strings which ran from the **soundbox** to the **pegbox** without passing directly over the **neck** and frets. Today, there are many models of electric guitar (and just a few **acoustic** designs) which have two necks (a few have three or even more), each of which has different strings. The most popular combinations are a six-string and a twelve-string neck or a six-string neck and a four-string bass neck. All these

This unique three-necked bass guitar has one fretless and two fretted necks, which gives it an interesting range of sounds

combinations give the player a bigger range of sounds. The violinist Shankar plays a double-necked electric violin.

A less elaborate development has been the addition of further strings to single-necked guitars and bass guitars. There are seven-string guitars, twelve-string guitars (with the strings arranged in six pairs), bass guitars with six or more strings and many other variations.

28

New classical strings

In the 1950s, the American composer Henry Brant asked the violin maker Dr Carleen Hutchins if she could re-design the stringed instruments used in classical music. This idea came about because, as each of the instruments had evolved slightly differently, the sizes and shapes of the four instruments were not properly in proportion. This meant that the instruments all had different **tones**, so that a viola, for example, sounded quite different from a violin, instead of simply having the same sound at a lower **pitch**. Dr Hutchins designed a family of eight new instruments. The smallest was a **treble** violin, pitched an **octave** above a normal violin, while the largest was a **contrabass** violin, which had the same lowest note as a double bass, but which had a much larger body, giving a fuller, richer tone. The instruments were praised by many musicians, including the famous conductor Leopold Stokowski (who featured in the animated Walt Disney film 'Fantasia'). While they are not widely used, the designs of the instruments are still being refined, and interested musicians continue to use them.

Dr Carleen Hutchins's new string instrument designs were the first innovation in classical strings for 200 years.

Strings, sampling and synthesis

It is possible to use many string instruments to 'trigger' electronically created (synthesized) or stored (sampled) sounds, by using a special **pickup** system. This converts the sound of the instrument into computer data using a computer language called **MIDI** (musical instrument digital interface). The performance artist Laurie Anderson has also used a violin in this way.

29

Glossary

acoustic referring to sound; also means 'unamplified'

amplify/amplification to make louder

avant-garde modern and experimental

Baroque a cultural period in Europe covering the 17th and 18th centuries

bass the lowest range of notes in general use (contrabass and subcontrabass are lower still)

bouzouki a Greek fretted instrument

bow a stick with a length of rosined hair attached which is used for playing certain stringed instruments

bridge a sharp vertical edge on a stringed instrument, over which the strings are stretched

Cajun a type of folk music played in the state of Louisiana in the USA

chamber chamber is the old word for room, so chamber groups are smaller than usual groups that play classical music

clavichord an instrument which has strings struck by metal hammers operated by a keyboard

concerto a piece of music written for an orchestra plus (usually) a single instrumental soloist

contrabass a pitch range lower than bass

dampers devices which muffle the sound of strings

drone strings strings which produce a single continuous note

electromagnetic pickups microphone-like devices which 'collect' the sound from an electric stringed instrument

ensemble a small group of (usually classical) musicians

fingerboard the surface of the neck of a stringed instrument, upon which the strings are held down to change the notes

frets/fretted small strips of metal, wood or gut on the fingerboard of a stringed instrument, across which the strings are held when changing the notes; having frets

Gaelic referring to Irish (or occasionally Scottish) culture or language

gears toothed wheels which transmit movement

gourd a rounded plant which can be dried and hollowed for use in instrument-building

harmonics extra notes which can be heard mixed in with a main note

headstock the part of a guitar on which the tuning pegs (or 'machine heads') are usually fixed

lute a round-backed instrument which preceded the guitar

lyre a square, harp-like instrument

mandolin a small, steel-strung fretted instrument

MIDI stands for musical instrument digital interface; a type of computer language which allows some electronic instruments to exchange data with computers and with each other

mute to muffle or quieten a sound

neck the thin part of a stringed instrument along which the strings are stretched to allow the notes to be changed with the fingers

octave a series of eight whole notes

30

pegbox the part of a violin etc. onto which the tuning pegs are attached

pickups see 'electromagnetic pickups'

pitch how high or low a note is

pizzicato the action of plucking the strings of an orchestral stringed instrument (they are normally bowed)

plectrum a small, flat object used to pluck the strings of certain stringed instruments

psaltery an early zither

qanun a Turkish zither

repertoire the music written for particular instruments, voices or groups

resonator a hollow object or structure used to amplify the sound of an instrument

rosin a sticky substance applied to the hair on a bow, allowing it to produce friction when drawn across an instrument's strings

solo/ist a section or piece of music featuring a single performer, or one performer alone; a musician playing such music

soundbox a hollow object or structure used to amplify the sound of an instrument

stopping raising the pitch of a string by holding it down at a point along its length

string quartet a classical ensemble which usually consists of two violins, a cello and a double-bass

sympathetic strings strings which are not played directly but which make a sound by picking up vibrations from other strings

symphony orchestra the largest type of classical orchestra

tailpiece the part on the body of some stringed instruments onto which the strings are fixed

tension tightness

tone the quality of a sound, often described in visual terms – dark, bright, thin etc.

treble refers to high notes

vellum a type of very thin leather

virtuoso an exceptionally talented instrumentalist

West/ern used by musicologists to refer to the music of Europe and the English-speaking world

Index